Earthquake Season

Earthquake Season

Poems

Jessica Goodheart

WORD PRESS

Published by Word Press
P.O. Box 541106
Cincinnati, OH 45254-1106

Cover art: *Crypto Egypto*, guash pen, tempera and oil, by Laura Harrison.
Author photo: Roxane Auer
Book design: Ernesto Cuevas

Typeset in Mrs. Eaves Roman and Mrs. Eaves Petite Caps

ISBN: 9781934999974
LCCN: 2010927724

Poetry Editor: Kevin Walzer
Business Editor: Lori Jareo

Visit us on the web at www.word-press.com

To my mother, Pat Goodheart

and to my father, Eugene Goodheart

Acknowledgments

Many thanks to the editors of the following publications in which some of these poems first appeared: *Antioch Review, Blue Arc West: An Anthology of California Poets, Cider Press Review, Free Lunch, Mudfish, Partisan Review, Pearl, Rattle, Salamander, Solo* and *Spillway.*

"Advice for a Stegosaurus" was published in the *Antioch Review*, Vol. 63, No. 4, Fall 2005 and is reprinted by permission of the Editors. Copyright © 2005 by the Antioch Review, Inc. The poem was also reprinted in *The Best American Poetry 2005* (Scribner), *Holt Elements of Literature, Third Course* (Holt Rinehart and Winston, June 30, 2008), and *Master Class: The Poetry Mystique* (Duende Books, 2009).

After appearing in *Cider Press Review*, "Earthquake Season" was reprinted in *Open Windows: Selections from the Winners of Poetry in the Windows*, 1995-2003 (Arroyo Arts Collective), edited by Suzanne Lummis.

Thanks are especially due to those who helped make these poems better, beginning with a brilliant teacher, Suzanne Lummis, and members of her Thursday night workshop. Deborah Landau has been a continual source of encouragement and good counsel. Molly Peacock's generous and insightful comments helped make this book as good as it could be. Many thanks go to Laura Harrison who produced the haunting and luminous painting that appears on the book's cover and to Ernesto Cuevas for the book's design. Allan Jalon's workshop at Beyond Baroque launched me on this journey. Eugene Goodheart read through the final manuscript and made me work a little harder. I am grateful to John Medearis, whose excellent poetic instincts and steadfast support helped me finish this book, and to Max Medearis for ten years of instruction and inspiration.

Contents

One

Advice for a Stegosaurus

Never mind the asteroid,
the hot throat of the volcano,
a sun that daily drops into the void.

Comb the drying riverbed for drink.
Strut your bird-hipped body.
Practice a lizard grin. Don't think.

Stretch out your tail. Walk, as you must,
in a slow deliberate gait.
Don't look back, Dinosaur. Dust is dust.

You'll leave your bones, your fossil feet
and armored eye-lids.
Put your chin to the wind. Eat what you eat.

War for Breakfast

Metal on metal
smoke or ash.
I eye the specials:
anthrax vaccine,
depleted uranium,
grenade launchers.
On the wall:
photos of boys,
their hair cut short.
Tabs unpaid,
they went off
to die as heroes.
The man at the table
next to me wants the man
at the table next to him
dead. I grumble to the waitress:
I did not order this.
All attitude with her
refugee eyes
and missing hand,
she tells me
That's what there is, honey.
The food is cold, I say.
She says, *Winter is colder.*

Earthquake Season

We can hardly tell anymore
whether the earth's trembling wakes us
or my seismometer heart.

Sometimes your aftershock footsteps
make me cry out. I'm not talking
about anything as trivial as the sun
but the loss of it.

What if I die without you
on the greasy tiles of a Taco Bell
in that radioactive light
where no one ever hopes
to look beautiful?

And yet this morning,
the floor rocked me
gently to the breakfast table
and you were there
with sunlight on the cactus.
And the only death I found
buried deep in the paper
as if beneath the collapse
of a house: a boy not yet fourteen
shot in the neck
under an open sky.

Let's Say I Find This Beautiful

Woman in nun's habit
strolling Vegas' old
strip, beer in hand, pavement
gray sky. 6 a.m.

20-feet-high, electric,
the billboard cowboy
and a real-live tumble weed
rolling down Freemont Street.

A Salvadoran man hawks wigwams,
sequined girlie t's, lucky dice
large as a sugar bowl.

Let's say I find this beautiful.

Even the 7-Eleven marquee
flashes psychedelic.

The magic man
on the video screen
cuts off his arm.
But it's still there.

Let's say I find

a couple of bleary up-all-night
faces, bodies like the dying
walking hand in hand
past the Bargain Mart

                    beautiful.

Let's say

a waitress in pink high heels
my second daiquiri

      Let's say

she's stuffing her pockets full
for two bedrooms, a pool,
the baby inside her,

nicotine-veined, his hands
still two little mitts

feeling their way
into fingers.

After Touching Down

The man seated in 22B cannot speak in words.
He makes the sound of a smooth landing,
like the boy he once was, the boy he is now.

His hands ride the updraft his mouth has made.
Then, fingers first, they plunge into a darkness even our pilot—
with his upbeat forecasts and sun-dipped vowels—knows is there.

In a stage-sized gesture, the man wipes his forehead, relief.
Tired, packed-in, ready for open spaces,
we do not smile at him or wipe our brows.

So four times more, he enacts the safe landing,
all 100 tons, the godly geometry of it.
Four more times, disaster movie-style: the crash.

His prayer hands turn upside down and inside out.
He's teaching us something, this man, about probability,
something we suspect but dare not say.

Tails we go down, into a night of scattered parts and fire.
Heads — wheels on the tarmac, crescendo of arrival —
and we are on the scarred earth.

A Dry Cleaner's Love Song

The air was filled with chemicals.
The fan blew acrid and cool.
His love for her was a great big drum,
a gaseous, dizzying pool.

She clasped his fingers, pulled at his sleeve,
said, "Let me live again.
My past is like a house fire
that singed my delicate skin."

"Lie flat for me, lie flat," he said.
"I'll press you crisp and smooth.
Your tired eyes, your cracked, scarred hands
will be mended, made like new."

He knew cures for careless lives
for girls led astray.
His hands were rough as a sailor's,
his eyes the color of clay.

"Speak of the past. Don't speak of the past.
I can see it on your dress:
stains of mascara, gin and tears.
Hush, No need to confess."

"I long for a love, a simple
love, a love of me as I am. "
But he pinned her down to his steel steam iron
and grabbed her soft, white hand.

"Shut your eyes, now shut them tight,
the gun will steam you clean.
The peroxide, the oxalic acid
is but a temporary sting."

Round and round she went
but the stains would not fall out.
And love, like a stain, once set,
hangs on, is difficult to rout.

The air still fills with chemicals.
The fan blows acrid and cool.
They make love in a great big drum
a gaseous, dizzying pool.

Mother of the Groom

Her leg swelling, she can hardly stand
to watch the wafer, the breaking of the glass,
Catholic priest and Jewish prayers. She can't reconcile
the boy who toddled after her
and this one drifting down the aisle
with the glazed look of a devotee.

As he draws near, her eyes redden and burn.
She remembers how they stuffed her into her parent's Ford
like a kidnap victim, the white taffeta
filling the entire back seat, then married her
to the boy's father, one of many
mistakes, this one immortalized
in photographs, one after another,
gentle slaps to the face.

And now the boy fills his lungs
with the sacred air of church,
gazes at his bride,
pinned to the altar as she was,
more fabric than flesh.

Let Go

No one ever doubted it was Eve's
mouth on the fruit's white flesh.

Still they watched the security camera tape
over and over, chins perched in judgment,

as though they'd flipped the lid
to their own dark souls.

Friday, words on crisp paper
announced: *To dust they shall return.*

The next week, no one ate anything
grown from seed, no one plucked

anything, not even an eye brow.
Down the long corridors, doors snapped

shut for private conversations
about Eve. We always knew.

There was something about her hands
how they stroked every surface

how they never came to rest.
One of the frames, frozen and tacked

to the message board, revealed a shadow
of a man, not the Adam they remembered,

the blessed one, always
in the full sunlight of his gleaming teeth.

No, this stranger sucked hungrily
on the sweet, hard end

of what he could not have.

Ten Cars Veered Off the Freeway and Up My Leg

It's no way to live, a four-car
pileup at the base of my spine,
overheated radiators steaming at my toes,
a carbon monoxide haze all around,
no time to sleep or love.

If I could shower this minute,
make my skin slick like the roads after rain,
one by one they'd skid, slide
off my body, scraps of colored metal
collecting with the hair in the drain.

In My Dream

You are already the disappointed child,
complaining about the tight, wet,
low rent crawl space,
your egg head and militant arms held high.

The nerve—
to use my body as a chute,
bulleting out, swinging
from the cord between my legs
damp and screaming,
like a monkey in a monsoon.

With you still dangling,
I make my way to a street
filled with fire engines.
Geese, mad with fear,
riot in the red-exploding sky.
Wrapped in only a sheet,
I hail a cab.

Am picked up, instead,
by a man with a gun
mounted on the back of his truck.
He takes the long way,
points out his favorite filling stations,
stops for ice cream sodas.
I waddle after him, thinking
gone are the days
when I traveled light.

Caesarean

What's inside must stay inside,
what's outside should be smooth.

I despise a skin that tears, reminding us
of what's wet and red and can't be put back.

In the birth ward, one swipe of the knife,
and I split like a blood orange.

Strapped to the bed, spine pricked,
abdomen open wide,

they pulled you out, first one leg
then another.

I was not ready
to meet you this way,

womb resting on belly,
a pink island in a red pool.

I'd have preferred another setting
when we were both a little more

dignified, you not so blue and amphibious,
and me dressed, hair combed.

I'm your mother and I love you,
but you are like a swallowed nail surfacing.

If giving birth could be soft, like a rose
opening, the gradual blossom,

or hard, like plastic dolls—
heads pop on, heads pop off—

not this salty tangle of veins and tissue, this
flesh and blood.

Insomnia

He gets up, walks into the door.
She sits bolt upright. It's four
a.m. The room's not black enough,
covers are not vast enough.
As he settles back to sleep,
his body curves enough to keep
her from spiraling back and down
into night's lost and found.
This time he'd roused her from plains
of Africa. She may never go again.
Now the dream evaporates.
Street noise takes the place
of all that sun and open sky,
miles of quiet. Outside
sirens sound. A helicopter trolls
the streets for some poor soul,
breathing hard in an alleyway.
She could get up and wait for day,
but for mother on the fold-out couch,
baby in the crib, his arms stretched out.
The clock's red digits glare and click.
In two days, she'll be thirty-six.
She loves the man in the bed,
this continent they've made,
bereft of grass and sun-drenched wind,
but full of Thursday's dishes done, skin
on skin. Now the steady beat
of morning starts. It's feet
on the floor. Baby cries.
Water's in the pipes. They rise.

Daily Commute

We ride out of downtown on a river of exhaust,
past a woman, drunk with the fumes,

who clutches a sign in dirty hands:
Very hungry. Please help.

Once I stopped to explain why we dress in steel,
point our chins east.

She shook her head, unwilling
to know a world outside her sorrow,

and I don't stop any more. She doesn't understand
the flow of traffic, the agreement we've made to move in sync.

Sometimes she holds out a bouquet of roses,
as if she wanted to jam the freeways with her troubled flowers,

but we keep going, drifting on rafts of glass
towards our half-painted houses

cats round in the windows
dry-tongued and hungry-eyed.

Two

Adam Eats the Beach

Adam wears a beard of drool and sand,
and raises his arms to the setting sun.
The wind's fingers take his face in hand.

Now his baby fists are plunging fast toward land;
he clutches the gritty floor, and with one
hand, evens out his old-man's beard of sand.

Seagulls huddled nearby disperse and fan
out along the coast. They're all to Adam
who sways like silk in the wind's hand.

He reaches toward a bird until a man
and dog pass by. Then gulls are done.
Dog is everything, vaster than sky or sand.

But night clamps down with its pink band.
A woman dusts him off. Her son
remakes the beard of drool and sand
before she plucks him from the wind's hand.

Facts on the Ground

With his seven good legs,

      Daddy Long hobbles through the wood chips

under a hail of pebbles, gray like gun fire,

      while ten-fingered Gabriel—darker than his twin

pockets full of broken glass, poison berries, nails

      rusty as a shipwreck—mans the low-slung oak of Bellevue Park.

When the spider stops twitching,

      the boys squeeze the necks of Coke bottles

broken and jagged, a jack o' lantern's smile.

      The mothers are round like watermelons.
      Their faces the cool hard skin.
      Their words wet with juice.
      They come along once in a great while
      smelling like plowed fields
      and put a stop to this.

But first Gabriel bends back the tree's slender finger

      until it snaps.

For a boy like that, a pine cone's a key,

      a stick a dagger, a brick a warning.

You see, it starts with metaphor

      and ends in the sand pits with

boys, many of them my brothers,

      and red eyes and treason.

And not just boys either.

On the Way to the Downtown Eye Clinic

His mother leads him by the elbow
past the sunburned amputee,
past secretaries on cigarette break,
through the roar of the jackhammer.
Hurry! she says, and pulls.

Out of the crush of sidewalk traffic,
the face of an old woman emerges, one eye
permanently rolled to white,
like a television stuck between stations,
neither seeing nor resting,
like what could happen to you, Fernando!
He's paralyzed.

The face of the lady rises,
higher than office towers,
her good eye bearing down on him,
her useless one like cloud cover
turning the afternoon gray.

Mamá! The boy runs and stumbles,
finds his mother's round hips,
grabs her skirt like reins and goes.

Fumigation

Barred from your home,
you wander the neighborhood, an outcast,
find coffee houses too loud.
Alone at a neon green diner,
you eat, feet suspended,
as roaches scuttle beneath them.

You stroll past your building,
shrouded in striped canvas.
Can it be that nothing inside lives?
He anticipated this, felt
the asthmatic's panic for air,
a tightness in his lungs.

Imagine a return to rooms
without oxygen or touch,
sleeping alone amidst poisoned sheets,
still and cold, like the sarcophagus
of a woman wronged,
as the gray morning light
casts shadows on the white walls.

When the gas dissipates,
you open your front door,
shaking loose the corpses of termites.
For days after, you'll sweep them up—
remnants of this latest infestation—
into a dry, black heap.

Instructions for the House Sitter

I.

To be thrown in the black container:
carcasses picked clean,
torn blouses,
knives bent beyond repair.
Always the trash collectors come
with their early Tuesday morning reproaches.
Pay them no mind.

2.

Best not interfere with the plants.
They are engaged in a civil war,
root against root. Daily, vegetation
comes into this world unnamed.

3.

Ignore the alarm that sounds nightly,
the Doppler effect from sirens approaching,
the police officers with their
nightsticks and clean shaves.
They will ask for the code.
It is *Judas*. Do not tell them.

4.

Refill the dog's dish in the evening.
But do not walk him unless
you are prepared to go as he does,
on all fours, weathering hours of solitude.

5.

The cat, once out of the house,
will climb to the neighbor's roof.
You will hear him cry.
He cannot get down.
The rain will start,
winds will tear down the power lines,
the whole hillside will go dark.

Refrigerator Day

in the full bright air conditioned hum
of my refrigerator day
are moments of triumphant scouring
call it progress

moments too when I want to
throw down my sponge and doze
curled up on kitchen tiles
letting mold grow green and wild

Day Spent Shopping for Lamps

The chandelier is a bride
in an emptying banquet hall,
drunk on her own dazzle,
weeping glass tears as she watches
the last guests head for the door.

The first woman race car driver:
a desk lamp. Ambitious in black helmet,
she revs her engine, flashes
her high beams and takes off

while fluorescent light,
unwanted roommate,
eavesdrops on phone calls,
never asks, never knocks.

A day at the mall
and I crave black sky
but come home to
the incessant flash and blink,
sockets clenching
cords, dusty and tangled,
the weight of night's
electric clutter.

No Lemonade

A vendor with the face of a prophet
can only repeat this sad truth
in broken English, point to Very Cherry Soda,
and drop hot dogs into the hissing vat.
The thirsty man rages,
gestures sunward
while a girl in mermaid shoes
wails and waits in a line so long
I hold my breath and turn to stone.

My son so wants popcorn
that is both sweet and salty that
with a patience I've never seen
he waits behind the man
gone mad from waiting.

Later, asleep in his car seat,
he keeps his hand in the hard-won bag.
We jerk to a stop. Eyes shut,
he presses three kernels to his cheek.
One cleaves to his face
like petals clinging
to the pages of a book so that,

as if it is my job to do so,
I forgive the man with the wild arms,
the girl crying to sit down
and praise a line that curled
around a corner
and led a boy past wanting
to sleep as deep as this.

Three

Kaleidoscope

Let's call you childhood:
mother staircase backyard branches
kind as the suburbs.

You cradled me like jacks,
let me tumble on my head,
clenched my bleeding nose.

In winter, you divorced, remarried
and gave birth again
and in spring, still puffed up,

you fed me leftovers—
head in the Jell-O,
fists in the Rice Pilaf.

How soothing those slow, sun setting nights
when neighbors crept onto the lawn
and ice rattled in the glasses.

I'd run into the house and,
with a roar and a bump, thump-thump
down three flights of stairs.

A spinning top, I'd soon subside
and let the last hot breath go out
like so many doors opening at once.

About death you taught me, too,
with an aging Siamese
who loved the warm road.

At night I heard your cries,
sniffling red-nosed, red-eyed desperation,
and I knew and you,

exhausted in knowing,
wiped the entrails off your dress
and slept a while.

Washington Square Park

Only the pigeons remain unchanged,
the same gray suits, heads bobbing back and forth.
Everything else is twenty years older today.
Especially the babies, shuffling along in flip flops
beneath the wide arch, sucking
mango Bobas, cones of blackcherry
chocolate gelato. It makes them superstrong,
walking through Washington Square.
The babies are deciding between NYU and UVA
They can say such big words:
"matriculate," "hubris."
They still have a lot of skin.
But their heads have shrunk.
Their bellies are flatter.
They look as if they were about to blow out
giant birthday cake candles all in one breath.
I have never been much for babies.
Even now, twenty years older,
they seem to need so much care.
They need toys that ring and beep
and trips round and round the world.
Only yesterday, they toddled by me in this same park,
pushing toy strollers, saying *Mama, Mama!*
I hardly saw them then, as I shuffled by in my flip flops
my head full of milk.
You have to admit they have gained a lot of confidence.
In just one day!
Now it's time to clap for the babies.
What a good job!
How big you are!

Aunt Raven's 60th Birthday

He arrived dressed in a policeman's tight blue
suit, handcuffed you to your grandmother's Queen Anne
dining chair. You'd been a bad girl. This much was true.

His box boomed Rick James (*Superfreak*) and then
his shirt unsnapped. You laughed and clapped.
I blushed from my perch on a Victorian

footstool. As his bareness brushed your lap,
he seemed to hold in his gaze me – only twenty,
flushed with champagne, in a wrap-

around dress my mother bought me.
How I ended up front-row to this theater
of the flesh, this body oiled and toffee

brown, I did not know. But Aunt Raven, you were
unfazed and would not be upstaged. You sent
to your room my red-haired, older brother,

who, polite as a waiter, returned in a moment
with what you required: something leather and neatly
coiled – a whip. As always, dear Aunt, you meant

to shock and did. I can still hear your low chuckle, see
surprise spreading across the young man's face.
For weeks, he phoned, hoping to find your free

spirit still free. But you were in another place,
tending sweet green peas in pots, fat
August tomatoes, backyard peppers, blue lace

flowers. Dressed in a pink muumuu and a floppy hat,
you told me you would not call him back, as if
my question were indecent: *I'm much too old for that!*

Shopping with Raven

After pain therapy,
I drove you to the gourmet grocery store.
You cut in line at the meat counter,
pointed a thin, jeweled hand
at the most expensive steak.
Back home, you crumpled
like newspaper on fire.
I fell beneath your hollowed-out bones,
afraid they might break,
your hair, black feathers of a bird.
We lay in the driveway,
next to the Town Car.
Palms clawed at the ashen sky.
A neighbor, hunched in a bed
of tulips, took no notice.

The Wounded Chair

After my new brother moved in,
hair like a flame, he took a hatchet
to a chair in a room painted charcoal gray.
He wanted black. The chair
stood in for my mother,
who was not his mother.

Through childhood, the chair hunched
in the dark room, its wound full of splinters.
I liked to go there. My laces glowed
white in the purple of a black light
as boys tossed darts that hissed
and sank into a red eye.

At fourteen, he built a workbench,
and, soldering torch in hand,
bent hot silver to his will,
forged necklaces with coral dragon tongues,
love knot rings he'd clean,
if we asked, in an acid bath.

Now all the chairs in my brother's house
have velvet cushions.
The walls are white, white, white.
He's so gentle, a freckled Buddha.
I sometimes wonder
what he's done with the wounded chair.

When Diane Arbus Came to Dinner

My mother cinched her garter belt,
fastened her jade anklet, and
painted her bow tie mouth black.
Her breasts became a resting place for shadows.
The bare bulb swung wide
over the dining room table.
Sit, she said. *Eat*, she said,
primping her puff of dyed hair.
My transvestite brothers
sulked in the vestibule,
pale with their own face paint.
Back from the circus,
Father soothed his scorched throat with gin.
Last time you caught him in your flash, Diane,
flames tumbled down his silk shirt.

My Father and His Wife Shop for Cemetery Plots

On a windy Sunday,
you stroll past tombstones
with your wife and a salesman.

This spot will do, you tell him, under the willow.
Here. But will it?

Should you get down on your belly with the bees,
feel the tickle of cut grass,
the dirt in your nails, on your tongue?

It makes no difference.
Willow or duck pond. Lilies, asters, roses.
Soon, you'll be tooth, shard, and nail.
And some time this long-limbed,
upright woman will join you, bone on your bone.

Right now, you giggle together. It's a lark,
a walk down the path of "here lies,"
the laughable dead
somber as straight men
in a comedy routine, a vaudeville
of cold stone and beating heart.

Watertown Graveyard

The graveyard, though it's morning, smells of starlight
and, like old books, the tombstones keep their secrets
from what shrieks and blares and hooks the mind
to sadness: modern subdivisions of the dead, the green glare

of awful flowers. I like the way death looks here: wintry.
Black locust trees; grass the color of straw.
But Hayes McCurdy, if bones could dance, you'd tell
of children all in white, their eyes like frozen ponds.

The dead are not stone fruit but wine. It's true.
Age improves them. So why not, from the safety
of doorsteps, praise sleet-stained marble and make
a hearth of teeth, a necklace of another's pain?

Lament

He hates eugenia branches devouring his view,
bamboo that breaks the brick pathway
to his yard. Once, from his house, he could see land he owns,
a hilltop burial plot, his when he is dead.
He eyes the keeper of the trees, his neighbors,
and revs the engine of his long black car.

The young couple, just moved in, hate the car
that leaks black oil, but prune the trees that block the view
to make peace with the old man, their neighbor,
who pounds on the door, complains about the way
their rose bushes, some diseased, some dead,
reach over the fence and contaminate his own

shrubs, the ones he lovingly feeds, what he owns
otherwise destroyed by eugenia trees. In his car,
he races through hills and contemplates the dead,
ones he killed in war, a wife who did not view
their land as sacred. She gave a plot away
to their daughter, who, refusing to be his neighbor,

sold the land to these neighbors,
indifferent gardeners of ground he once owned.
He drops a note, a little poison, on their steps on his way
to the courthouse, slams the door to the car
that spews black fumes. He will restore his view;
for even when old friendships are dead,

daughter gone, wife and rose bush dead,
anger blooms. If these neighbors
will not understand his point of view
then a judge must make them own
up to their mistake, must take their car,
their house, their peace of mind away.

The woman who lives across the way
instructs the couple on how to keep their dead–
end road harmonious. Let him park the old car
where he may. Bring him wine. He wants neighbors
who are his friends. What he owns
is all he has. That is not the couple's view.

They let the trees obliterate his view. He'll lose his way,
they say, forget his own name, his daughter's face. Once he's dead,
new neighbors will replace him and his car.

After All

My tiny grandma shivers
in her flowered house dress.

I say, *Grandma,*
sit here
on the prongs of the fork.
Let me hold you over the fire.

Her legs dangling,
she says what she always says:
You are young. I am old.
You go out. I stay in.

Since I am the future, I go
up the tallest building in Manhattan,
bullet through subway tunnels,
and get as far as Brooklyn

before turning back
to Queens, where I find
Grandma still tiny
but charred,
unrecognizable.
My chest heaves madly.

Oh Grandma! Do not say I killed you
with neglect.
After all, even you sometimes forget.

Abuela

In this town, the dead walk with the living.
La llorona wails in the park for her lost children.
On these streets of the conquered,
I look for your old-world face.
You were Mexico to me,
my box of skeletons,
my cobblestone lady.
And now that I am here,
I mutter to you as I step off the narrow sidewalk
to let pass a woman wrapped
in faded scarves and bent.

I'm not Mexico. But Belz,
the Pale of Settlement,
ancient synagogues,
and shattered storefronts.

In a plaza of sculpted trees,
a girl, not more than sixteen,
sells painted turtles from a sack.
She wears your long, hard look
of disappointment. Abuela, tell me,
where did she find it?

In a Brooklyn tenement.
My brothers went to school.
I did the dishes. I slept last.

You believed only in books
without prayers,
gave me no edifice,
no Gothic spires. Abuelita,
why do you kneel here among the faithful?

In a Queens apartment,
friends who died stopped calling.
I read Wittgenstein's biography,
a dehydrating woman,
refusing to drink.

My shadow crawls past you
and up the steps of a gazebo.
From there, I see your horse-drawn town,
toppled tombstones in the Jewish cemetery.
It was too far to go
to watch your burial.
Yet I've come to where the sky falls hard
and clouds belt out thunderclaps all afternoon
to stand under stone arches
with this balloon vender
and his clutch of wild colors,
to wait for the rain to stop,
the wind to die.

Four

Vanishing

Did I tell you about our room, how it's growing smaller? Each day, we lose an inch, I figure.
It creeps up on you the way a perfectly lovely evening fades to night. At first, we thought
clutter made the room cramped. I put magazines at right angles, lined up lotions and
mascara like little soldiers. Life returned to almost normal. We even made love
once, bumping together in the hot, small room. The next time: too hot, too
small. Soon we were pushing the dresser into the hall, discarding plants
we'd nurtured from seed. People have made do with less: Dad, as
a kid, slept in the living room, Grandma always barging in on
him in the bathroom with fresh towels. Tried remodeling,
hired a company that organizes closets. But by the time
they arrived: walls only 3 ft apart husband after
me to lose weight no room for us both.
Since he left I feel better. Remarkable
how much room another person
can take. No furniture now but
when I sit with my back
against one wall feet
against the other I
form a per-
fect
V

In a Bucket

Knock myself stupid.
Thwack. Thwack.
Fish-mouthed. Can't get out.
Gills sweat red. Hook
lodged in slippery self,
flopping at a good fast pace.
Can't keep this
tempo up. Can't
warn others. Anyway,
who'd listen?

Like them,
I drank silver
and that was life.

Urgent Care

The television blinks cop shows and cold medicine.
A man doubles over, while another tries to burn

a hole in the wall with his eyes.
At 2 a.m., I doze, head in hand.

I awaken on a cart stacked high with Jell-O.
A rumpled orderly pushes me past cataract patients,

past colon cancer, past my mother's yogic breathing,
and my grandmother's last days.

There are so many doors marked *radioactive*,
so much white.

Down a hallway, my brother bends
over a microscope searching for lost time;

around the corner: my grandfather's subway heart attack,
the curious faces peering, peering;

and on the wall: an X-ray of someone's
fractured spine, perhaps mine.

Gliding through florescent corridors,
past years I'd forgotten:

gears shifting, dial tones, freeways,
refrigerator hum, a.m. radio.

They undress me, weigh me, stick needles in my arm.
The room shrieks like a siren.

Hush, the doctor is coming.
The nurse has brought cool cloths, a comb, a mirror.

An ancient face looks back at me:
hair like sleet, rivers of skin, and eyes I recognize.

Matryoshka

Whenever my grandfather's mother

    came dimly into the foreground of my imaginings,

she lay in a dark room, in a forgotten Ukrainian town.

    "Died" and "young" were the posts of her bed.

To the new world, my grandfather carried her bad news

    sold life insurance to Queens accountants, shopkeepers.

During visits to his apartment, I'd open a Russian doll

    down to the last original girl.

My father, obedient only child, kept her blood's secret,

    willed his way through top marks at school,

writing twelve books at last count. Finally, to me it came

    the sleeping genebaby until in my right breast

a raggedy flower bloomed. I was 37.

    I opened every doll until I found her

high gloss, eyes green like mine.

Matryoshka, how did it take you—a knot in the flesh,

the top hot part of a flame in the pit of the arm?

Tell me, before I pack you, mute and nameless,

into a hollow doll belly and inside another and another.

Someone Brought Me This

1.

As though I'd said too often:
this ho hum has got to stop.
So quiet. I can hear pallbearers
marching through the sticky streets.

Little candy in my chest.
Let it rest. Let it rest.

Look at my ivory child,
thin-hipped and perfect,
can't see beyond his own tomorrow.

A woman comes to my office
and cries. It's just candy, I tell her.
A hard bright sugary mass.

2.

The living are the great exception
like that woman hurrying now
through the waiting room, her blouse
skin-warm and shimmering.

3.

After the rains: forgetfulness.
Each drop a dead man
in the moist earth.
Children and short-legged dogs
run over the dirt
while I sit bald on
a weathered bench
and write these words:

How it grows. How it grows.
Pity like a red, red rose.

This is Not a Bill

For the moonscape inside you

      for little darts thrown at your finger tips.

For the heart's blood

      mixed eight times with poison

acacia, the yew tree

      the bark of the slow-growing yew.

This is not for the workshop in Salt Lake

      where they sent your bones.

For the month you slept in the reclining chair

      arms too tender for touch.

Not for the weight of the car door, taste of the pedal

      the stop and start of it.

Or for the miles of tubing wrapped twice around this earth.

      The trembling of rats in their silver houses.

This is not a bill

      for the stink of the hyacinth

the bathroom of four walls, the leaves

      the polite applause of the leaves.

Not for the doorway of skin.

    The woman in white marching in.

For this paper we send now.

    This fine, black print.

Pay later.

On the Table

Kind man with the needle,
tell me I'm checking in to a fancy hotel.
You're my bellman
and this is not dangerous.
Take me to a room, all white,
Antarctica of the mind,
calm as cut flesh, cool
as street corner jazz.
Rise, let me, above this pandemonium
of men and cutlery
hassle of arteries and paperwork,
this fine refrigeration.
Nothing like rest
and what is this if
not a sweet, narcotic sleep,
the perfect alibi.
If, during this time,
blue flames blacken
the copper underside
of an empty pot
and during this time
a boy wants me to spell wizard
with the eighteen letters of his name
then show them the sign on the door.
Do Not Disturb.
I'm in another country,
due back when the blackberries ripen.
Give me time. Even after
the click-click of seat belts
unlocking, I will be
not quite home,
a little red box of pain
rusty-hinged
can't open wider
than a mouth.

Elegy for a Fertility Symbol

The wind blew. Fire flickered.
I went to sleep.
Someone thought to burn you.

You popped and hissed
and in my dreams
an old pagan god
swayed to your music.

When I awoke, you were ash.
I had wanted to keep you
crackling in the flash
and smoke of my hearth

for the memory of the dance
its heady rhythms and salt
the damp silk
of bodies,
the space between them
black as wine.

Ten Minute Walk

These brief, bright days in the in-between
hard, sweet candy on the tongue.
Gift of broken flower pot
of bougainvillea pressing
lipstick to chain link
of this once again body of mine
sure-footing the rutted sidewalk.
Clutch of jungleflower, some preening, yellow,
others already spent,
thick tongues of a jade plant
drunk from the hard liquor
of this spring's rain.
Beyond the white fence,
the road curves into a green
mouth of leaves. A city skyline
of cool knives looms, promises.
Once, on this scrap of pavement,
I saw a mutt speckled brown
so thin that my index finger
and thumb could have taken
measure of her belly. I did not
bend down to help her
where she lay, stiff,
growling, her cloud eye
pivoting toward me.

Everyone is Asleep, No One is Home

you hear a pulse in your ear

and there is a way to dive

into it and you bask in the thrum

you live in the you-and-you a while

it's just a sometimes thing this earbeat this tapping

these fear buttons row up on row can tell you things

lead to passageways

you join a pulsatile flow a river

tour of hissing chirping brass bells and breaking glass

bands march through the cochlea

round hubs and switches

your thumb has a heartbeat and a neon will

and you and your thumb are one

you click through symptoms

it might be nothing it might be the end

you picture the blood chips the god sob

there's a man whose ear sound drove him mad

no one else could hear the devil humming

the refrigerator stalking him

so like a ruined king

he scratched his ears almost off

he's here with you now

on the limbs of a diagnostic tree

you might not come down

you need your dose of death

your fraternity of chatter heads

you can see what it adds up to no

you're diving remember

the held breath the muck

the deep-water

panic and pandemonium

of fraying cords and broken parts

but in a cage of sparks

you do emerge

full of the knowledge

it could happen to you it will happen to you

Prayer for a Return to the Ordinary

Let the days walk over us,
their heavy, certain tread.
Let us wind up tired, face to face
little to say.
Let us wash the plates clean,
eat supper hungrily, thankfully, not at all.
Let us wash the plates clean.
Give us taste of late autumn,
of June. Let the days grow long,
let them start hot
the sun hammering the parking lot,
the men outside waiting for work,
for the ordinary day.
Let the woman nourish her entourage of pigeons.
Let the barbed wire twist and glitter
around the gutted factories.
The newspapers, let them rend our hearts
and the man who delivers them,
let him move from house to house
in the wet morning as though invisible.
Let the dog, unfed and howling,
pull the chain and pull again.
Let churches people the sidewalk
Sunday after Sunday.
Let plants crave water
and darkness invite sleep.
Let the housekeeper's girl, all nerves,
stutter in her new language
and let her mother regard her
as something she will lose
Let that be her sadness.
Let the wide dark drink up the day,
day after day.

Let me feel where ribs meet,
where your back narrows.
Let the question
of what to do next hover,
the quietest angel.

My Doorman is a Poet in Need of Praise

He wears silk shirts under his blue doorman's jacket.
His knee never ceases to jiggle under the table of his night.

He lights imaginary cigarettes with the fire in his eyes.
Doors are like books that he opens

books that he closes. When we come in laughing
on Saturday nights he looks up at us

through the winters of the last century
his mind a full boat of immigrants.

With packets of coffee shop sugar, he builds temples
to an only-sometimes god. To the blue-bearded panhandler,

he offers coins from his childhood.
To the fourth-floor poodle salt biscuits of silence.

Mornings, he stands so that we may wrap him,
tree-like, in the colored lights of our praise.

All he asks is that we commit to memory
the luster of his brass buttons, the creased landscape

of his forehead, his tangled eyebrows,
his fingernails of amber.

He is not practical like the super, not rich like the owner,
does not squander words like the postman.

But when he greets us, the whole city
tips sideways and water drains from the alleyways.

Dear Chef

As truffle season approaches,
I look among the morning mail for your
Valentine menu, for red pepper pesto
and tender leeks, Art Deco cubes of truffle.

This time when the creamy card stock comes,
amid gas and electric bills,
and I read your italic
Come to Our Annual Truffle Dinner,
I will write you back.

I may be one on a mailing list of many
in my cramped kitchen, sniffing week-old cheese,
prying open cans of soup with rusty gears,
hungering for linen table cloths, a gentle touch
of saffron. But you are what I have.

I see you in a tall white hat,
cook's red face, metallic eyes,
in a kitchen spacious as the West,
counters like oceans and ten sous-chefs,

skimming kumquat citrus sauce
with silver spoon, slicing shallots
for crispy rings, whipping cream by hand
for lemon crepes with banana moussaline.

Hot with appetite, knowing what I must
forgo, I jostle the dirty dishes aside
to make room for my reply
with words you've taught me:

orange bitter
        tart with tender

sabayon and sorrow
        foie gras and wild mint

The Lost Notebook

I last saw it in a shopping cart with cross-eyed wheels.
Now half-finished stanzas run loose
among the vitamins,
sit shivering with the milk cartons.
What was in it? asks a clerk.

I try to remember: *A girl in a tattoo shop*
crying over her punctured skin.
The scab on her ankle blooms
in the shape of a flower.
He wrinkles his brow,
tries to picture the girl, the shop, the flower,
points me toward produce

where I find my mother,
careless as wind,
knocking the oranges from their bins
with her sizable hips.

Outside, a cashier on cigarette break
hasn't seen it either.
We try to keep the place clean.
It's a family market, she inhales
before forcing one shopping cart
down the throat of another.

The health inspector cannot abide
the seven ravens
who cluck and squawk at the meat counter.
He warns the manager:
Unfinished poems attract roaches.

My neighbors don't shop there anymore.
But I still wander the aisles,
drunk on salad dressing,
searching for band-aids pink as cats' tongues,
discounts on pickles jarred in brine.

The Tree of Houses

(by Paul Klee)

Come visit me in my tree of houses.
I spend most of the red year on the tallest
branch, a sphere rotating on my peaked roof.
From my door, from every window:
the star of David.
Sometimes, in my most tipsy house,
I watch the earthen sky,
or the beak of a falling bird
while chairs and cups
knock about the rooms.
Summers, I descend to the house
that is shaded by the Tree of Houses.
It is cool there. You'll like the faded door,
the floor that slopes and fills
with rain during summer storms.
The sun burns so hot that the tree's aflame.
But if a hand fans that fire, you can't tell.
Though red, it doesn't seem at all like hell.
Spear Lilies, Sedge Grass, Chinese Flame Trees.
Ladder to branch. Branch to ladder.
I've left a way for you to follow me.

Falling Asleep While Writing This Poem

If I can balance these words
        on the blue
        blue line
If I can bite my tongue my lip my lashes
        and the wind comes through
        and the wind is wet with rain
If like a giant cape my lungs expand
        and the air smells of rhubarb
        and you breathe out
If I rise and walk to the canyon floor
        and crows shriek off-key
        until the sky blinks shut
If I sit outside on the deck and rock
        and skunks come by for a midnight drink
        and not far off the coyotes wail
If I hold on like breath to your wiry body
        and not let go
        and not let go

Stick Your Head in the Copier

Let the light seep into your eye sockets,
your pores. Illuminate your hair
with a flash as bright as Vegas.

And you, the you that is not you, the inverse of you,
will be tacked on every cubicle wall
as a reminder of courage. *She took a chance,* they'll say.

Stuck her head into the jaws of the great machine.
(It terrifies all of us, its mysterious appetites
and blinking impartations.)

Of course, you may simply be tossed
into the wastebasket, which gorges from nine to five
on a bleached coleslaw of trees.

Or recycled into a romance novel,
teeming with breathless heiresses and dark-eyed suitors,
your cracked lips and shadow hair barely recognizable.

In any case, you'll have felt the light in your veins.
For a moment, you'll have glowed like a saint.

About the Author

Los Angeles poet Jessica Goodheart was born and raised
in Boston, Massachusetts, attended Columbia College,
and earned a Master's degree in urban planning from
the University of California, Los Angeles. She's worked as
a park ranger, a telemarketer, a journalist and, for the past 13
years, as a researcher for an advocacy organization dedicated to
building a fair economy. Her work has appeared in
The Best American Poetry, *The Antioch Review*, *Blue Arc West: An Anthology
of California Poets*, *Mudfish*, *Salamander*, *Cider Press Review*, *Pearl* and other
journals. Her poems were featured in the Poetry in the Windows
exhibit, sponsored by the Arroyo Arts Collective in Los Angeles.
In 1999, she was selected to read in the annual *Newer Poets* series,
sponsored by the Los Angeles Poetry Festival and Beyond Baroque.